First published 2025

Copyright © Leesa Reading 2025

The right of Leesa Reading to be identified as the author of this work has been asserted in accordance with the Copyright, Designs & Patents Act 1988.

All rights reserved. No part of this book may be reproduced, stored in a retrieval system, or transmitted in any form or by any means, digital, electronic, electrostatic, magnetic tape, mechanical, photocopying, recording or otherwise, without the written permission of the copyright holder.

Published under licence by Brown Dog Books and
The Self-Publishing Partnership Ltd, 10b Greenway Farm, Bath Rd,
Wick, nr. Bath BS30 5RL, UK

www.selfpublishingpartnership.co.uk

ISBN printed book: 978-1-83952-881-1
ISBN e-book: 978-1-83952-882-8

Cover design by Andrew Prescott
Internal design by Andrew Easton

Printed and bound in the UK

This book is printed on FSC® certified paper

Memories, Tribute, Grief, Pet Loss & Support

MAX
One in a Million

Leesa Reading

DEDICATION

I dedicate this book to my beloved Max, and all the other dogs who've crossed the rainbow bridge.

CONTENTS

About Max	9
A bit about me	13
What happened	15
What I miss	18
Memories/things Max loved	19
How Max helped me	21
Things I did to help myself	22
Why is the human-dog bond so strong?	25
What are the 5 stages of grief?	26
Ways/tips to help you recover and heal	28
Star breathing	29
Poem	31
Rainbow bridge poem	32
How long does it take to grieve?	34
What to do with their belongings	35
Poem	36
Things I experienced after Max passed	37
How to help your other dog/pets	38
Helping your child/children through this difficult time	39
Should I get another dog?	41
The anniversaries of firsts	42

Selfcare alternative therapies	43
Soul dog	45
Letter to Max	47
Things you can say to someone who is grieving their dog	48
Things you can do for someone who is grieving their dog	50
How grieving affects the body and mind	52
Key points about grief	53
Does grief ever completely go away?	54
Space to write down some things about your dog	55
Mantras	58
Is crying a good coping mechanism?	60
Neurodivergent people and grief	61
Dear Max/last day envisions	62
Doggy donut recipe	63
The end	65
Additional help and support	68

ABOUT MAX

Max was a white, red and brown Border Collie, fur so silky and soft. With beautiful brown eyes (so human-like). He was born on the 22nd of April 2011. We got him the old-fashioned way, from the newspaper (before we knew anything about breeders). Max was my first dog. We were meant to have one of the black and white puppies advertised from the litter, but the breeder gave us a white, red and brown puppy instead, and we didn't question it as it was all so surreal at the time. I'm so glad we got him though, as I truly believe it was meant to be. We were a perfect match, he was nervous, and we think he was probably the runt of the litter. I'm a nervous girl myself so we matched well.

Max and I understood and helped one another. He was very timid and shy on the first day at his forever home with us, but he soon came out of his shell with all the love and affection he was given by all of us. All we had for him at the time was a child's bowl, a towel for a blanket and some fluffy car dice we found for him to play with, which he ended up absolutely loving playing with. We had nothing prepared as we got him much earlier than we thought. But we soon bought everything for him shortly after, and he was still carrying his fluffy dice around with him. It was July, and I had the week off work for my birthday, which worked out perfect timing as I got to spend the whole week settling Max in and spending every moment with him. Max was so cute, such a small, adorable, floppy legged puppy. The sweetest, perfect precious little paws, with the most beautiful fluffy face ever.

Having this new responsibility and new routine felt amazing, it was so rewarding, and just what I needed without even knowing it at the time. Max came into my life exactly when I needed him, and we bonded so quickly, and he soon became my absolute world! Max loved his food and walks equally as much. We live next to fields with lots of wooded areas, and we loved exploring and going on adventures together over there. Sometimes we would go to the field behind the back of our house and take his football with us. He loved running back and forth chasing his ball in the field; he would stay out there all day if he could.

When I had to go back to work, I would make sure to get up early and walk Max in the morning before I started my shift. At lunchtime I would come home for my break so I could then again walk him over the field. He helped me get through my day at work, and I'd be counting down the hours until I finished so I could get back home to him to spend time with him and take him out again. We had to start spelling the word O-U-T eventually as Max was so clever and picked up words super-fast! Some other words he knew like F-O-O-D and B-A-T-H, to name a few. Max also knew lots of tricks and commands, such as 'Sit', 'Give a paw', 'High five', 'Down', 'Spin around', 'Cuddle', and 'Bark' on command'. He even knew my parents and my names.

Max was a lover of many things, 'purple thing' being his favourite. It was a round comfort teddy, that we weren't quite sure which animal it was supposed to be, and therefore ended up being called 'purple thing'. We would say, 'Where's your purple thing?' and he knew exactly what we meant and went to grab it every time. He also loved his 'dinner winner' that was a chew stick that he'd have at dinner time. Ice cream was another favourite of his. I used to make little frozen yogurt pots for him to lick when it was hot. For his birthday I'd give him an ice cream cone and he'd demolish it in seconds. Every Sunday Max would have his own little roast dinner, even with vegetables. He loved broccoli, peas and carrots the most. Max loved peanut butter, too. He enjoyed licking it from a spoon and on his lickimat. Max needed lots of mental stimulation and we'd play lots of puzzle activity toys and enrichment games. He loved sniffing for treats in his snuffle mats, playing in his ball pit and digging in his sand pit. Max loved spending lots of time out in the garden, playing football, fetch with his nerf tennis ball launcher, and he especially loved playing 'the DO DO DO game'. It was a game I made up where I'd throw and hide treats around the room or in the garden, singing 'DO DO DO DO DO DO,' and Max would run around finding the treats. His tail would wag faster the quicker I sang.

Max loved to lay in the garden watching the birds fly by, soaking in the sun and sniffing the fresh air. He also loved the snow and experienced it many times. We used to make snowmen, and one time he walked his lead through one and accidentally chopped off the snowman's head. It was hilarious and it was moments like these I'll never forget. He brought me lots of laughter. Presents were another thing Max enjoyed, tearing the paper used to bring him so much joy. Every birthday and Christmas I would wrap lots of toys and treats for him to open. He'd also help my family and me to open ours, too. Picnics in the fields or in the garden were another thing Max and I loved doing. Eating from party plates whilst sitting on the blanket. Autumn was our favourite season, early misty morning walks through the crunchy leaves together. Max truly was one of a kind, such a special soul that came into my life when I needed him. He got me through my days.

A BIT ABOUT ME

A bit about me here. I worked as a qualified pharmacy dispenser for the NHS for many years. I enjoyed my job dispensing prescriptions and making dosette boxes, helping customers with their medication. Unfortunately, I got forced to quit my job by an inconsiderate, unprofessional co-worker. This is when Max gave me the inspiration to start making healthy dog treats for him. That later became the start of my new venture, my small business called Maximillion's Munchies. I made a website and shared my products on there. I then branched out and sold my treats at local stalls, markets and dog shows. As time went along, I came up with more ideas and incorporated dog paw and nose balm, snuffle mats, and bandanas. Of course, Max modelled for me and taste tested all the treats in which he gave his paw of approval. Peanut butter is one of his favourite things, after all. Up to now I have sent my treats all over the world including America, Australia and Belgium. Also, I now stock my treats in a local shop, too. This is a big achievement for me and something I never imagined.

Max has helped me in so many ways, even with my mental health, too. I struggle with anxiety, panic attacks, and low moods. Max would help by giving me the motivation to get up and out every day for walks. He was my emotional support dog, my therapy, my best friend. Our bond was so strong, he was always by my side comforting me. My shadow, my protector. My world.

I started writing this book by journalling. I wanted a way I could remember Max. That is when I decided it would be a good idea to write a book as an outlet to help me grieve. When you're grieving it is hard to remember the good things, and I wanted somewhere I could put it all down on paper so I could look back and remember it all, whilst making a dedication to Max, too. Through all of this I am also hoping to help other people who may be grieving for their dog.

Some people may not understand that a dog is more than just a pet. A dog is family. A child to some, best friends to others. A strong bond. A companion like no other.

WHAT HAPPENED

After spending 11 years of my life with Max, for him to be suddenly gone just doesn't feel real. It's not fair. He should still be here with us. I'm still finding it very hard to process that he's no longer here. Max had a seizure Friday morning, the 27th of May 2022. We rushed him to the vet's and had to leave him there to be cared for. All morning into the afternoon he was there with an IV drip and on sedating medication. Later that day we spoke to the vet, and we were told some tests had been done on Max and his heart came back ok, his kidneys, however, were failing, and it looked very likely he had a brain tumour. Come 8 o'clock that day we went to pick Max up and bring him home, which gave me hope, to be honest. We were told with special food, kidney failure may not be a problem for now, and if the tumour doesn't turn then that also may not be an issue for the time being. We were told to take him back into the vet's in the morning to see how he got on. This felt like some relief, and we were on the understanding that when the sedation wore off completely, we were on the road to recovery and had plenty more time. Unfortunately, my worst nightmare happened; at 12pm that night Max suddenly passed away. I'm heartbroken. I was stroking his head and telling him I loved him. Trying to hold it together. I was scared. A feeling like nothing I've ever experienced before. The thing I held onto was Max got to come home and see all of us. Spend some time with us. In his home comforts. He rested in his favourite spot, with his pillow and blankets. I really felt like he held on to be at home with us.

The pain and emptiness remain to this very day. I am struggling to adjust to life without Max. I have constant reminders of him everywhere I go. There is not a single day that goes by when I don't cry and think of him. 'Until we meet again, beautiful boy.' Max is laid to rest in the garden where he loved being. He's underneath a tree, with a rose bush coming over the top. The tree is full of decorations. There are paw print solar lights going around the front. A slate photo on the ground. Lots of flowers. A bench to sit on next to him with an engraved plaque of his name. It brings me comfort that he is home, and close so I can visit him every day.

Max is laid to rest with his purple thing, strawberry teddy and his blanket covered in rainbows. Just after Max left, a robin started visiting me every day. It may sound cliché, but I truly take comfort in believing it's Max, and it's his way of telling me he's ok and at peace. All through summer to winter the robin has been visiting. He sits on the branch directly above Max's tree, still to this day. Some other signs I found comfort in, the white butterfly that used to fly near me whenever I was in the garden. The white feathers that drifted down from the sky, and the brightest rainbow that shone on Max's birthday. Thank you, Max, for sending me these signs. I love you.

I have many pictures and ornaments of Max in my home. I have a big box frame displayed on the mantel piece, with Max's collar, pawprint, photo and snippet of fur inside. I found comfort in making photo frames, personalizing candles, painting pebbles and buying tree decorations for his memorial. I also named a star after him. It helped to keep me busy and, in a way, feeling like I was letting Max know I was thinking of him.

WHAT I MISS

Max, I miss you. I miss your beautiful face. Your scent. The way you felt so silky and soft when I cuddled you. The love I felt when you looked into my eyes. How your tail wagged when I sang to you. The noise of your collar dinging. Your tippy tappy paws when you walked along the floor. Your squeaks and barks, and even your farts. Holding your paw. Laying with you. Kissing your fluffy face. Petting you. Sharing my food with you. The way you licked my tears away when I was sad. Playing games with you. Our adventures in the snow. Walking with you. Sitting in the garden sunbathing with you. Looking up at the stars and moon with you. Teaching you tricks. Giving you treats. Giving you presents. The excitement on your face when I got home. Your comfort. Your safety. Your love. I miss you being my best friend, my loyal companion.

MEMORIES/THINGS MAX LOVED

Playing fetch with his nerf tennis ball launcher in the garden. When it snowed, he couldn't find the ball and his tail would wag fast, whilst he sniffed around trying to find it. He'd turn around when he found the ball and his cute little nose would be covered in snow. When I made a snowman, Max would knock it over by accident and eat the carrot and buttons I used to decorate it. Spending time in the garden sunbathing, in his spot upon the grass in the corner and in his teepee. When we walked to the bluebell field, it was beautiful, and he sniffed all the flowers and then did a wee on them. Classic. When Max got excited when we saw the goats and horses on our walks, but if I fed the horses apples, he barked at them. Walking over the bridge in the woods, Max did a funny walk over it. All the picnics we shared; Max loved the little paper party plates. He would have a party ring and some popcorn as a treat when it was his birthday. When we got Max an ice cream from the ice cream van one time, he watched out of the window licking his lips then demolished it in no time. Max loved his carob dog advent calendar; he would lick and lick the one square for ages. He loved ham, his red Kong bone filled with gravy bones.

Being brushed. Sharing my rich tea biscuits in the morning with my cup of tea after he went for his walk. Lover of squirty cream, roast dinners, and peanut butter. Every birthday Max would get a small pork pie, and I'd put a number candle in it.

The way Max opened the door with his nose and grabbed his toy in his mouth. He used to eat his chews with both paws like a human. When he ate something yummy, he rubbed his nose with his paws. When it rained and he got wet, I'd towel dry him, and he would run along the hallway shuffling his bum, so funny! When his farts made him jump and he'd run off from them. Playing with his chewed-up ball pit balls. Playing with his games like a pro. He'd work them out real fast. When it rained hard, and I'd open the back door for him, he'd run straight over and catch the drips in his mouth. How his head tilted when I spoke to him and said his favourite words. The way Max walked around the house with his treat ball. Max was such a character. Truly one in a million.

HOW MAX HELPED ME

Max still managed to help me even after he was gone. I started having grief counselling to help me cope with the massive loss of him. After a short while of having weekly sessions, my counsellor recognized me displaying symptoms that led me to getting a diagnosis that I never imagined. I filled in questionnaires, had the assessment, and it was confirmed. I was diagnosed with ADHD. It was hard accepting and processing this at first, but I started to learn more about the condition. Things started to finally make sense. All the anxiety, low moods, emotional regulation, overthinking, worrying, executive dysfunction, rejection sensitive dysphoria, sensory issues, sleep problems - the list goes on - all had a reason now. I thank Max for leading me down this path. I may never have known otherwise.

THINGS I DID TO HELP MYSELF

Things I did that helped me: I got two tattoos in Max's memory, one was a letter 'M' coloured in with the colours of the rainbow, representing the rainbow bridge. The other one was a robin holding a love heart in its mouth, representing the robin that visits. I let off a helium balloon up into the sky for his first birthday. I had a cushion made with a photo of Max printed on it so I could cuddle it. I bought flowers, lit candles, and decorated his tree. I wrote a note and took it to where Max used to love walking. I got a silver necklace made with his fur inside a star pendant. I printed out many photos and made a scrap book.

If you're reading this book, chances are you may have lost your dog, too. I just want to say, keep talking about them. Let yourself feel all the emotions. Let those tears out and cry as much as you need. Know that it wasn't your fault, you loved them dearly. Try not to let the guilt eat you up. Cherish all the memories you had together.

Because: *'What we once enjoyed, we can never lose. All that we love deeply becomes part of us.'*

HELEN KELLER

Max, you are one in a million. You made me a better person. You were my best friend. You never judged me. You were always happy to see me and spend time with me. You didn't care what I wore, or what I looked like, you just loved me for me. I'll love you forever. Loving you changed my life. Losing you did the same. You were the reason I went vegan. You were my purpose. You were the best dog I could ever wish for.

WHY IS THE HUMAN-DOG BOND SO STRONG?

The same bond a mother would feel with her child. Our oxytocin levels increase when we gaze into our dog's eyes, and the love hormones help us to create that mother-child bond. That is why losing your dog is equally as painful as losing a child/loved one. Also, our dog is always there by our side, getting involved with everything we do, and we spend more time with them than most people.

WHAT ARE THE 5 STAGES OF GRIEF?

1. Denial
2. Anger
3. Bargaining
4. Depression
5. Acceptance

Denial is a coping mechanism that our brain uses to protect us. A way of avoiding trauma and our emotions. We don't want to accept what has just happened or believe it is true.

Anger can come from the guilt and emotions we have built up. You may feel angry at yourself because you feel you could have done more or done something differently perhaps. Or even to the closest people around you, or even the vet.

Bargaining. You may feel irritable or stressed, going over every scenario in your head. You may believe if you did things differently, went to the vets sooner, picked up on something earlier and so forth, that the outcome may have been different.

Depression is the stage of grieving that tends to last the longest. You may experience feelings of hopelessness, intense sadness, crying, numbness, a feeling of 'What's the point?' Low motivation, low mood, and sleep disruption.

Acceptance is the final stage of grief. You start to acknowledge your loss and that things have changed, and life will be different now. You start to move forward, and things start to feel a bit easier. This does not mean that you will not experience any feelings of grief again. The process is a rollercoaster, and the emotions come in waves. You may, however, feel it gets a little less heavy over time.

These emotions are perfectly normal. Never feel ashamed to allow them. I couldn't stop crying after losing Max. This is very common immediately after a death, as our bodies are processing the shock and loss and helping us to reduce the overwhelming experience we are going through. It may differ for some people; they may display numbness and be unable to let out their emotions and cry. This is normal, too. Guilt is also a normal response after losing our loved one. Our brain is trying to make sense out of what has just happened. As a result of this we tend to blame ourselves. I found that the feelings of guilt subsided slowly but gradually over time. I was also feeling very lost. A part of me, my daily routine and responsibilities, had changed significantly. I noticed a change in my sleep pattern, a lack of appetite and my motivation. This also got easier with time. As cliché as it sounds, time is a healer. It never goes away, but over time you adjust, and it becomes easier to live with.

WAYS/TIPS TO HELP YOU RECOVER AND HEAL

Here are some ideas to help with your loss. I found these things helpful:

1. Allowing yourself to feel your emotions, trying not to block them out
2. Making a memorial/scattering ashes in a favourite spot
3. Making time to rest
4. Talking to a counsellor/therapist
5. Buying things to decorate a tree/plant a tree
6. Pebble painting/being creative/scrapbooking
7. Getting a tattoo
8. Getting a personalized photo cushion made online to cuddle
9. Getting a necklace made with their fur/ashes inside
10. Still talking to them at their place of rest
11. Lighting candles
12. Smelling their belongings, a blanket or soft toy, for example
13. Watching videos of them
14. Name a star after them
15. Keep talking about them, using their name
16. Breathing techniques

STAR BREATHING

This involves either imagining a star shape in your mind or you can trace a star shape with a pencil on some paper. You start at the top by going clockwise around the star and then follow the instructions below. On each hold, you hold your breath for 4 seconds. Breathe in through your nose and out through your mouth. Have a try for yourself! It really helps.

Deep breathing helped me lots. Deep breaths stimulate your parasympathetic nervous system. It kept me feeling grounded and calm. Especially when panic would set in. It can also help relieve tension and to bring our mind into the present moment.

POEM

Max, when I look up in the sky,
I look for you in clouds passing by

When it rains, I hear the drops,
Picturing you and missing you lots

When the sun is shining down,
I look for you laying on the ground

When I go to sleep at night,
I imagine holding you so tight

Thanks for sending us the robin,
It makes me smile, yet starts me sobbing

You are always on my mind,
Memories can never be left behind

I'll love you always and forever,
Until we can be back together

It helps me to think you're with your purple thing,
I know how much comfort it did bring

RAINBOW BRIDGE POEM

RAINBOW BRIDGE (FROM YOUR DOG)

When you feel sad and lonely, and all you want is me
Just place a hand upon your heart and know that's where I'll be

I know how much you're hurting but remember me and smile
I know we are apart right now but its only for a while

Please take comfort that I'm happy where the sky is always blue
I'll be waiting at the rainbow bridge when heaven calls for you

'No one ever told me that grief felt so like fear'
                                                              CS LEWIS

Grief is like the sea; it comes in waves. Some days are harder than others. Be extra kind to yourself on those days. Some days I can speak about Max and smile, but some days I get choked up just thinking about him or saying his name. It's hard to accept Max is gone and never coming back.

'I think we dream so we don't have to be apart for so long. If were in each other's dreams, we can be together all the time'
                                                              AA MILNE

HOW LONG DOES IT TAKE TO GRIEVE?

Well, that can vary for each person. Some people may start to feel better in weeks or months. For some people it may take years. No amount of time is right or wrong. You take as long as you need. Whichever way, it's important to allow the process to unfold naturally. Keep talking about your dog, still using their name. I found this to be a comfort as I still want to say his name out loud, and for it not to be a sore subject people don't like mentioning. Remember grief is not a weakness, it's love with nowhere to go.

'How lucky I am to have something that makes saying goodbye so hard'

AA MILNE

WHAT TO DO WITH THEIR BELONGINGS?

For me I wanted to keep absolutely everything of Max's. It also took me a very long time to move his things - some of which I still haven't. I have some of his toys on a shelf and his lead is still hanging in its place. I will never let go of his belongings. For some people, though, I understand they may not have the storage space, or it may be too much seeing their belongings constantly.

You may want to give their belongings to friends or family, or even donate them to a local rescue centre to help other dogs in need. Either way, do what feels right for you. If you just wanted to keep a few things like a blanket, an item of clothing or a bandana, for example, you could get them made into a memory bear online. Also, you could put their collar and a photo in a box frame with a favourite toy or ball inside.

POEM

When the sun comes up tomorrow, and your heart is torn in two
Know that I sit beside you in everything you do

The years we gave each other can never be erased
Hold onto those memories throughout the darker days

I know the time will come again when you will walk with me
Until then, know I'm happy to be running fast and free

THINGS I EXPERIENCED AFTER MAX PASSED

I still felt his presence, and on a few occasions, I heard his collar tags jingling. I'd sometimes look over the room and see a shadow in his spot. I felt I could smell his scent sometimes, too. Apparently, this is normal to experience during the grief period. So, try not to worry. I found it somewhat comforting. If a death is sudden or traumatic, it's your brain's way to process what has just happened. You may experience flashbacks, too. If you are finding this difficult to deal with, you may benefit from seeking out a medical professional for some help and support at this time.

HOW TO HELP YOUR OTHER DOG/PETS

I didn't have another dog or pet, and I could only imagine how they must be affected, feeling and grieving too. I did some research to add here to help you and your other dog or pet.

1. Be patient and compassionate
2. Stick to their routine as much as possible
3. Give them extra love and cuddles
4. Plenty of mental stimulation and playing games
5. Do not punish them if they become destructive

Remember they have just lost their friend, their playmate and companion, too.

Be sure to contact your vet or a dog trainer/behaviourist for extra support if your dog shows any unusual behaviour or alarming signs.

HELPING YOUR CHILD/ CHILDREN THROUGH THIS DIFFICULT TIME

Again, I don't personally have any children, so I've done a little research to help.

Breaking the news to your child is going to be difficult. Allow them to express their emotions, whether it be crying or getting angry. Comfort them as much as possible, and let them ask questions, by answering them according to your child's age.

Here are some examples of things you could say to your child:

1. Our dog is in heaven now
2. Our dog is no longer in pain
3. We did everything we could
4. Our dog loved us, and they knew we loved them deeply
5. Our dog is at peace now
6. We will always love and cherish them
7. They will always be in our memories

8. It's ok to be upset, encourage them to express their feelings and emotions
9. Tell them you are here for them

Always encourage your child to talk about their beloved dog or pet, still using the dog's name.

Let them lay flowers or decorate a tree, paint a pebble or draw a picture. Letting them get involved can be beneficial to them. If your child walked the dog with you, maybe you could still walk your usual route to keep up their routine. You could also buy them a memory bear or a personalized bracelet for them to wear.

SHOULD I GET ANOTHER DOG?

You may be thinking, 'Should I get another dog?' or 'When will be the best time to get another dog?' The truth is no one answer fits all for this question. The time scale will vary, some people find the silence is too much to deal with and the distraction of a new dog will help them, so they may get one straight away. For others, they might wait months or even years. Some may never want to get another dog again. This will differ for each individual person. Whichever you decide is up to you. You will simply just know when or if the time is right for you. If you're unsure, maybe helping at your local rescue centre could help, if you're not ready to make that commitment yet. Or walking or looking after a family member or friend's dog for a short while may help.

THE ANNIVERSARIES/YEAR OF FIRSTS

The first year after you lose your dog, like their first birthday, gotcha day, first Christmas without them will be very difficult. It awakens your grief and is another painful reminder you no longer have them by your side to celebrate with. I was one of those over-the-top pet parents. I would wrap presents, make a birthday cake, buy lots of things and take lots of photos. I miss it all. It helps me to still mark these occasions by letting off a balloon or buying some flowers. There might be some people who, on the other hand, may not want to honour their dog on these occasions and that's also fine. Again, it's about doing what feels right for you.

Here are some other ways you could mark the occasion if you want to, but you're unsure how:

1. Light a candle
2. Visit their place of rest
3. Get a memorial tattoo
4. Donate to a rescue or animal charity
5. Re-walk your old route
6. Decorate a tree
7. Look through photos and videos

SELF-CARE/ALTERNATIVE THERAPIES

Here are some things that can be helpful after you lose your dog and during the grieving process:

1. Speaking with a counsellor/therapist
2. Practising breathing exercises
3. Eating a balanced/healthy diet
4. Any form of exercise/yoga
5. Trying to get enough sleep
6. Keeping to a daily routine
7. Grounding exercises
8. Crystal healing
9. Meditation
10. Mantras
11. Writing in a journal
12. Online groups
13. Listening to music
14. Gardening
15. Arts and crafts
16. Baking

17. Speaking to people/expressing your emotions
18. Walking
19. Fresh air
20. Consult your doctor/medication

It is very important during times of grief to take care of yourself and your wellbeing, even though it may feel hard to do at the time. Self-care is crucial for the mind and body. Not all these things may work for you, but it's about finding which self-care practice helps and benefits you.

SOUL DOG

What is a soul dog?

A soul dog is a bond and connection you share with your dog that is different from a regular bond with a dog. You feel a deeper, closer, spiritual, emotional bond with them. Both you and your dog can feel this. Many people say it is a once in a lifetime bond. It is believed your soul dog came into your life for a reason, whether it's to understand the true meaning of life, love, connection or purpose. You evolve with each other, and they shape who you become. This is why losing your dog is so difficult, especially if they were your 'soul dog'. Nobody else except you and your dog knew just how big the bond and connection were between you both.

Here are some signs you had/have a soul dog:

1. SOUL CONNECTION

You feel a deep connection with your dog, and the bond feels special. You truly believe they were meant to be in your life.

2. DEEP UNDERSTANDING

You and your dog feel you have a deep understanding of each other. You both know what the other one feels and needs.

3. INSEPARABLE

You crave your dog's presence and company. When you are apart you miss them lots. You miss the familiarity and connection you share. You find it hard to leave them when you go out. You can't wait to get home to see them.

4. TRUST

You share trust, feel safe and calm when you are together. You comfort each other.

LETTER TO MAX

Dear my beloved Max

I hope you knew just how much I loved you, and how much of an impact you had on my life. I wish you were still here with me. You were the best thing that ever happened to me. You will always remain a big part of my life. I will always talk about you and share our precious memories. I cherished our time together. You were my best friend, my loyal companion. My purpose. Thank you for choosing me. I will be forever grateful.

All my love

Leesa (Mummy)

THINGS YOU CAN SAY TO SOMEONE WHO IS GRIEVING THEIR DOG/PET

My deepest condolences for your loss. I know how much you and (pet's name) loved each other.

I'm so sorry you are going through this. When you are ready to talk, I would love to hear about (pet's name).

They will always live on in your memories.

It's beautiful how you and (pet's name) found each other.

You were the most caring and loving owner.

I can only imagine what you are going through. Please know I am here if you want to talk or spend time with me.

Grief counselling or therapy may benefit you in this difficult time.

It's ok to feel your emotions.

I'm sending you all my love.

Let me know if there is anything I can do.

THINGS YOU CAN DO FOR SOMEONE WHO IS GRIEVING THEIR DOG/PET

Check in on them.

Offer to make them food, as they are probably not thinking of eating or have the motivation to cook. Getting a little shopping in for them may be a good idea, too.

Offer to clean, tidy, empty the bins or any chore they may be finding difficult to keep on top of at this difficult time.

Offer them support and be someone they can talk to when they feel ready.

Suggest grief counselling, therapy or online grief groups.

Encourage them to write in a journal as an outlet, as they may not be feeling up to talking.

Encourage them to go outdoors every day, even for a short while. Walking and fresh air can be beneficial for their wellbeing.

Make sure they get enough sleep. If they are finding it difficult to sleep, recommend natural remedies such as lavender pillow spray or chamomile night time teas. Relaxing music or white noise can help with relaxation, too. Consult a doctor for advice or medication if they're really struggling.

Don't give up on them. Even though they may seem withdrawn, quiet, uninterested or snappy, make sure to be there for them and include them in things.

A hug really wouldn't go amiss, showing them you are literally a shoulder to cry on.

HOW GRIEVING AFFECTS THE BODY AND MIND

Grieving takes a toll on the body as well as the mind. Aside from stress, anxiety or panic attacks, it can affect your immune system, give you stomach upset, fatigue, create issues with muscle tension, and affect your sleeping patterns. When you grieve your body produces extra amounts of stress hormones which contribute to all of this. The brain regions affected by grief are the prefrontal cortex, the thinking part of the brain, the anterior cingulate part that is responsible for emotional regulation and the amygdala. The prefrontal cortex and anterior cingulate are underactive and the fear centre of the brain becomes overactive. The brain interprets grief as emotional trauma or PTSD. This is the brain's response to grief. This can last from weeks to months. Research has also shown that inflammation is linked to grief. If you have any existing conditions such as arthritis, it can make it worse during this time. Taking time to be active every day can help relieve some of these symptoms. Grief can also lower your immune system, and you may be more prone to colds and viruses. Keeping on top of your vitamins, especially vitamin C, and keeping hydrated can help.

KEY POINTS ABOUT GRIEF

Grief is a normal response to losing a pet or loved one

Grief is painful

Grief comes in waves

Grief affects everyone differently

Grief affects you mentally and physically

Grief changes you

Grief is a part of life

DOES GRIEF EVER COMPLETELY GO AWAY?

The answer is 'No', grief doesn't completely go. It does, however, lessen in intensity over time. It's impossible to forget about someone who had such a big impact on your life. Grief is love with nowhere to go. It's not uncommon for you to stop engaging in things you once enjoyed. Guilt, or lack of motivation, can contribute to this. As time goes along most people find they adapt to their grief and return to a new kind of normal. You will start to find pleasure in things again and possibly even new things, too. Some things may still trigger your grief such as smells, certain objects, food, places or songs, for example. Grief is like the ocean; it comes in waves.

SPACE TO WRITE DOWN SOME THINGS ABOUT YOUR DOG

Here is some space for you to write down some things about your dog. It's beneficial to write things down to help with the grieving process. It can be easier than to say them out loud. Also, when you're grieving it's harder to remember things, especially the good things. You can look back here at any time.

Write 3 things you loved about your dog:

1
2
3

Write 3 things you miss about your dog:

1
2
3

Write 3 things your dog loved doing:

1
2
3

Write 3 of your dog's favourite treats or toys:

1
2
3

Write 3 words to describe your dog:

1
2
3

My favourite memories with you:

Your favourite places:

Things about you that made me smile/laugh:

How you made me feel:

If I could tell you one thing now:

Write any additional things about your dog here:

MANTRAS

I am allowed to grieve.

I allow myself to feel my emotions.

There is no timeline on grief.

I am strong, even when faced with loss.

I am surrounded with support and love.

It is ok for me to feel both sadness and moments of joy.

I am worthy of compassion and support.

I can find peace and healing after my loss.

The power of affirmations for grief are positive statements that can help you with your thoughts and emotions. Incorporating these affirmations (mantras) into your daily routine can be beneficial to your wellbeing. You could set a reminder on your phone to make a specific time each day to say your affirmations. In the morning when you wake up may be best, so you can start your day on a positive note. By consistently practising, you can create a better mindset.

IS CRYING A GOOD COPING MECHANISM?

Yes, crying can help improve your mood. It releases oxytocin and endogenous opioids, also known as endorphins. Once released your body may give you a sense of calm and self-soothing. This helps to lower stress levels. It's important to cry. It's not healthy for you to keep it all built up inside. Crying can also let people know you need support.

A BIT ABOUT NEURODIVERGENT PEOPLE AND GRIEF.

Neurodiverse people may find it more difficult to express their emotions. The emotions of grief can therefore intensify already existing symptoms such as emotional dysregulation. Neurodiverse people tend to process and express emotions more intensely than a neurotypical person would. It can be more overwhelming and difficult to cope with. It could also take longer to grieve. Being extra compassionate and understanding to yourself or to a loved one is crucial during this time.

DEAR MAX/LAST DAY ENVISIONS

Dear Max

This isn't how I imagined it would be when I thought of your last day. I planned the day to be filled with all your favourite things. I wanted to wrap lots of presents for you to open. I was going to get you a cheeseburger and an ice cream from McDonalds for dinner. Cook you a steak, followed by pancakes for tea. I wanted to take you to the field you loved and lay there with you taking in our surroundings, with a little picnic, using those party plates you liked. Making sure to take lots of photos and videos of us together. I wanted to give you all the cuddles and kisses in the world, telling you how much I loved you, whilst gazing into your beautiful brown eyes. I wanted to create a paw print picture. I wanted to spend time sitting in the garden with you and everyone who loved you in your favourite spot on the grass, surrounded by your favourite toys and cozy blankets all warm and snuggled, holding your paw with you feeling at ease, with the sound of the birds and the fresh air blowing on your face. Peacefully, safe and relaxed.

DOGGY DONUT RECIPE

(MAX'S FAVOURITE HOMEMADE TREATS)

Makes x4 donuts

Ingredients:
1 cup of rice flour
1 tablespoon of peanut butter (xylitol free)
½ cup of water
4 chunks of carob
1 tablespoon of desiccated coconut

Method:
Mix flour and water together in a bowl, until the dough is formed.
Add peanut butter and mix until all the dough is the same colour and there are no lumps.
Roll the dough out with a rolling pin.
Cut with a circular cookie cutter, using a smaller circled cutter for the donut hole in the middle.

Place the donuts onto a greaseproof lined baking tray at 180 degrees for 25 minutes.

Bake until golden brown.

Leave to cool for 30 minutes.

Melt carob either in the microwave in a suitable dish, or on the hob until fully melted.

Dip the donuts into the melted carob and sprinkle with desiccated coconut.

Leave to cool for a further 20 minutes.

Then serve to your dog as a treat.

Always make sure to have fresh drinking water available.

Keep the treats in a cool/dry area away from direct sunlight or heaters.

The treats will last for 3-4 weeks if stored correctly. Or they can be dehydrated for a longer shelf life of 6 months.

LINKS:

INSTAGRAM - Maximillions_munchies
FACEBOOK – Maximillions munchies

END

I would like to thank you, firstly for buying my book, and secondly for taking the time to read it. I hope you somewhat enjoyed hearing about Max. I also hope that this book has helped you or somebody you know with their grieving process and all the stages that come with it. My intention for this book started out as a journal, to help me grieve and to remember all the memories Max gave me. Along the process I decided it would be a great way to help and support other people who may be experiencing grief and the loss of their loved one, too.

I'm wishing you all the very best on your healing journey.

May all your memories of your four-legged friend live on.

A little mention and thanks to my parents, they were a big part of Max's life too.

ADDITIONAL HELP AND SUPPORT

The Samaritans - 116 123
Animal Samaritans pet bereavement service – 0203 745 9859
MIND - 0300 102 1234
Blue Cross pet loss support - 0800 096 6606

Your doctor

Counselling directory

Online groups on Facebook
www.animalsamaritans.org.uk
www.samaritans.org
www.mind.org.uk
www.bluecross.org.uk

(If you are really struggling and having suicidal thoughts, make sure to seek help immediately)

To infinity and beyond Moo Moo's.

2011–2022